Alphonso Wetmore

Soldier, Adventurer, and Writer

Mary Barile

Truman State University Press
Kirksville, Missouri

Notable ★★★★★ Missourians

Copyright © 2015 Truman State University Press, Kirksville, Missouri, 63501
All rights reserved
tsup.truman.edu

Cover art: Chester Harding, portrait of Alonzo [Alphonso] Wetmore (1793–1848), oil,
ca. 1821, courtesy of Missouri History Museum, (#1962.149.1).

Cover design: Teresa Wheeler

Library of Congress Cataloging-in-Publication Data

Barile, Mary.
Alphonso Wetmore : soldier, adventurer, and writer / Mary Barile.
      pages cm – (Notable Missourians)
Audience: Ages 10 to 12.
Includes bibliographical references and index.
ISBN 978-1-61248-147-0 (library binding : alkaline paper) — ISBN 978-1-61248-148-7
(e-book) 1. Wetmore, Alphonso, 1793-1849—Juvenile literature. 2. Missouri—Biogra-
phy—Juvenile literature. 3. Soldiers—United States—Biography—Juvenile literature.
4. United States—History—War of 1812—Biography—Juvenile literature. 5. Soldiers—
Missouri—Biography—Juvenile literature. 6. Explorers—Missouri—Biography—Juve-
nile literature. 7. Explorers—West (U.S.)—Biography—Juvenile literature. 8. Authors,
American—Biography—Juvenile literature. I. Title.
F466.W47B27 2015
973.5'2092–dc23
[B]
                                                            2015012032

Contents

Introduction

In the early 1800s, Americans began to move from the eastern states into the wild, mostly unsettled lands west of the Mississippi River. These emigrants were looking for rich land and a new life on the American frontier. Many were also looking for adventure.

One of these emigrants was an army officer named Alphonso Wetmore. Despite losing his arm in the War of 1812, Alphonso remained in the army and joined an expedition to explore the lands west of St. Louis and establish forts in the new territory.

After the expedition ended, Alphonso was stationed at a fort on the frontier. He wrote and published stories about his many adventures. After leaving the army, Alphonso worked as a lawyer and newspaper publisher, wrote plays and stories, and traveled on the Santa Fe Trail to trade in Mexico. He also compiled a book called a "gazetteer" that told people in the East about Missouri and encouraged them to move west and settle in the new state.

Alphonso Wetmore joined the army because he wanted a life of adventure. He found excitement, and left many stories that tell us about his life and journeys on the frontier.

chapter 1

Frontier Childhood

Alphonso Wetmore was born February 17, 1793, in the rural town of Winchester, Connecticut. He came from a large family; he had nine brothers and sisters. Alphonso's name was probably a little unusual for that time, but his parents must have liked unique names. He had sisters named Lois Malinda and Artemesia and brothers named Pythagoras and Salmon.

Alphonso's parents were from New England. His father, Seth, had been a soldier during the American Revolution. In early America, only men who owned land or paid taxes were allowed to vote. Some people, including Seth, argued that every man, rich or poor, should have the right to vote. Wealthy Connecticut landowners did not like that idea and often threatened people who wanted to expand voting rights. In 1803, when Alphonso was ten years old, Seth and his friends moved their families to New York, looking for a better life and the chance to own land and vote.

To get to their new home, the Wetmore family and some of their friends traveled along the Mohawk pike, a rough road that cut through the wilderness to western New York. The emigrants settled in the

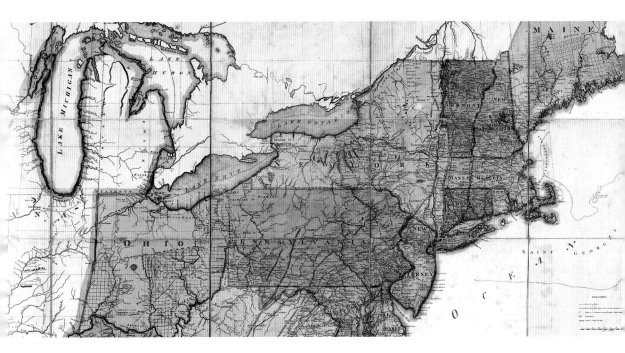

By the early 1800s, the United States had sixteen states, extending as far west as Ohio. The areas that were newer and less settled were considered the frontier.

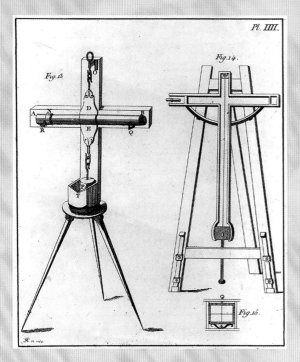

As settlers established farms and set up towns, they needed to know where one person's property ended and another person's property started. Surveyors measured and mapped areas so people would know where boundaries were.

small village of Ames. The village had been established in 1779 by people from New England and was located next to an Iroquois village. When the Wetmores moved there, Ames was on the United States' western frontier. Americans were moving into the area and establishing farms. In Ames, Seth worked as a land surveyor and sheriff, keeping the peace and caring for his family.

The frontier of western New York was wild and life was not easy. Bear, cougar, and bobcat roamed the woods, and winters were very long and very, very cold. The first Wetmore home may have been a log cabin or a small wooden house. Few people had glass windows because window glass was expensive and it was hard to transport glass in wagons without breaking it. So windows were usually small and did not let in much light. The downstairs may have been one large room or two smaller rooms.

Most log cabins had an open area upstairs, which was called a loft, where the children slept. People used clay and other materials to seal up the cracks between the logs, but it didn't always work very well. Some pioneers told stories about how during a winter storm, the wind blew snow through the cracks and people woke up in the morning covered with a cold, white snow "blanket."

Alphonso's family raised vegetables, grain, and fruit trees. The whole family worked hard, starting before the sun rose and ending the day by candlelight. Most families kept cows for milk and the girls would churn the cream into butter. The Wetmore children were expected to help with chores like planting, weeding, hunting, and fishing. Putting food on the table took a lot of time and energy. In the fall, families prepared for the winter by drying beans and fruit and storing grain and root vegetables, like potatoes.

Even when a farmer had a good harvest, it was difficult to store enough food to last until they could start growing food again the next spring. Springtime was often called "the six weeks' want" because people had no fresh food and were waiting for the new crops.

Grains like rye and corn had to be ground into flour before they could be made into bread, and a

Gristmills were usually located on streams, where the flowing water could make the water wheel turn. The water wheel was connected by a series of big gears to stones that turned and ground the grain into flour.

farmer might have to travel a long way to take his grain to a gristmill. People often went without bread for weeks when they had used up their flour and couldn't get to the gristmill.

Besides raising crops and preparing the meals, Alphonso's mother also wove fabric from wool or flax (fabric made from flax is called linen) and sewed the family's clothes, a big job for her large family.

Alphonso and his brothers and sisters worked hard to help the family succeed. The children did their chores, but they also had to study. There are no records that tell about

A New York writer

Washington Irving, the author of "The Legend of Sleepy Hollow" and "Rip Van Winkle," was famous in America and Europe. He was from New York's Hudson Valley, but in 1832 he visited Missouri. He wanted to see the great prairies before they disappeared. He also wanted to visit with Native Americans. Irving stopped in St. Louis and visited with Governor William Clark before continuing west. He later wrote *A Tour of the Prairies* describing his adventures.

Alphonso's schooling. Like many children, he and his brothers and sisters may have been taught at home by their parents. Or Alphonso might have traveled to distant Albany, New York, and attended school there. Later in his life, Alphonso said that when he was young, he read plays by William Shakespeare and books by Washington Irving, his favorite author.

For a young boy on the frontier, Alphonso was well educated and his future was bright. He even studied to be a lawyer, but instead of setting up a law practice, Alphonso joined the army in 1812.

Fibers from the flax plant are very strong. Fabric woven from flax fibers is called linen, which is a strong and durable fabric that can last for many decades.

Chapter 2

A Soldier in the War of 1812

In 1776, the colonies declared their independence from England. It took seven years for the Americans to defeat the British, and the war ended in 1783. The United States was finally independent, but England and the United States continued to have conflicts over borders and trade.

By the early 1800s, American settlers were moving to settle west of the Appalachian Mountains. But the British had forts in those areas to keep Americans out of Canada, which was a British colony. Native Americans were also concerned about protecting their lands, and the British sometimes gave them supplies. At the same time, England was at war with France and wanted to stop the United States from trading with France.

Soon Americans began to worry about a new war with England, and thousands of Americans

joined the army. Nineteen-year-old Alphonso Wetmore was one of them. The slim, red-haired young man was a skilled marksman with a pistol and rifle. In March 1812, he became a lieutenant in the infantry. These men were also

Soldiers' uniforms were made from wool and their summer underclothes were made of linen. They had to keep their uniforms clean and neat, which was not easy.

The town of Queenston Heights was on the Niagara River between Lake Erie and Lake Ontario in present-day Ontario, Canada. American forces crossed the river and attacked the British forces stationed at Queenston Heights.

known as "foot soldiers" because they marched and fought on land.

After they joined the army, Alphonso and his friend Robert Morris were sent out as recruiters to sign up new soldiers. At that time, the friends were both courting a pretty and accomplished young woman named Mary Smith. Mary owned a miniature painting of herself and Alphonso and Robert both wanted it as a mark of her love.

The two friends decided to play a game to see which of them would get the painting. Alphonso won the game and got the portrait. He told Mary he would always carry her portrait in a pocket over his heart.

The conflicts between the United States and England got worse, and in June 1812, President James Madison declared war on England. This was the War of 1812. In the United States, some people called it the Second War of Independence.

Alphonso and Robert were sent to the Niagara frontier between New York and Canada, where the British had many troops. On the morning of October 13, 1812, they joined nearly three thousand men who crossed the Niagara River and attacked

Some soldiers had families who lived with them at their fort. Betsy Doyle was married to a private in an artillery regiment at Fort Niagara. When the fort was under attack, Betsy helped by carrying hot cannonballs from a furnace to the soldiers who loaded them into the cannons. When a hot cannonball hit its target, it would start a fire.

the British troops in Queenston Heights.

During the battle, Alphonso was hit by pieces from a cannonball and seriously injured. Another soldier carried him to a nearby farmhouse and found a doctor. The doctor saved Alphonso's life, but Alphonso's right arm had to be amputated.

Despite this terrible event, Alphonso was luckier than many other soldiers. The Americans lost the Battle of Queenston Heights and many men died, including Alphonso's friend Robert Morris.

The War of 1812 in Missouri

The War of 1812 ended in 1814 when the Americans and the British signed the Treaty of Ghent, but fighting continued in the Missouri Territory between Americans and the Sauk Native Americans, who had allied with the British. In May 1815, a band of Sauk attacked American soldiers near Cuivre River, in what came to be known as the Battle of the Sink Hole. In 1816, the Sauk's leader, Black Hawk, finally made peace with the United States government.

Alphonso returned home to recover from his injuries. He proposed to Mary Smith, and they married in 1813. Alphonso didn't let the loss of his arm stop him. He learned to write and to fire a pistol

Dolley Madison was famous for her gracious manners and skills in entertaining different kinds of people. By hosting social events, she added to the popularity of her husband, President James Madison. She is the first president's wife to be referred to as the "first lady."

with his left hand, and learned to ride a horse with one hand.

In a few months, Alphonso returned to his regiment on the Canadian border. He was made the paymaster for his regiment, which meant he was responsible for transporting large amounts of money and making sure the soldiers in his regiment were paid. Despite dangerous travel, often in bad weather, Alphonso did his job well, and he was promoted to captain and then to major.

The war ended in 1814, but Alphonso remained in the army and was stationed along the Canadian border in upstate New York. Mary joined him there and they started a family.

Like Alphonso's parents, he and Mary chose unusual names for their children. While they lived in New York, Alphonso and Mary had three sons: Diogenes, Leonidas, and Thaddeus.

After the war, Alphonso was visiting Washington DC and was invited to dine with President Madison and the first lady, Dolley Madison. Mrs. Madison asked Alphonso about his experiences in the war, and Alphonso told her about the battle in which he was injured. He said that the only reason he lived was because Mary's portrait, placed in a pocket over his heart, stopped the bullet.

In fall 1818, Alphonso was with the Sixth Infantry Regiment when it received orders that changed the Wetmores' lives forever. Alphonso's regiment was going to join the Yellowstone Expedition and travel up the Missouri River to establish forts on the western frontier. Alphonso and Mary were moving to the Missouri Territory.

Chapter 3

Life on the Frontier

For some soldiers, traveling west with the regiment meant leaving their families behind. But Alphonso was an officer and officers were allowed to have their families travel with them and live near where they were posted. So the Wetmore family traveled with the troops across land and by river to reach St. Louis. Many other officers' wives and children also followed the army to new homes in the Missouri Territory.

Travel down the river to St. Louis could be dangerous. The soldiers and their families traveled by keelboat, a large flat wooden boat that was moved along by the river's current, sometimes helped by sails. When the current was slow or the wind was still, the men pushed the boat along with long poles.

Keelboats were used mostly for carrying freight, so there were no special cabins for passengers. People traveling by keelboat ate, slept, and cooked on the open decks. They had to be careful with cooking fires, because the boats were made out of wood.

Alphonso later told stories of his family's journey to the western frontier of Missouri. Besides soldiers and families, the Wetmores' keelboat also carried military supplies. One day, someone left hot ashes from a campfire on the deck and the wooden planks

Keelboats were narrow and long with flat bottoms so they could travel in shallow rivers. Because they flowed with the current, they could only be used to travel downstream.

caught on fire. As the flames moved toward the barrels of gunpowder, Alphonso gave the alarm. The keelboat's crew came running and threw buckets of water onto the fire. Alphonso's warning and the crew's quick actions saved the day.

There were other dangers to traveling on a keelboat with a flat open deck. One day, a woman passenger fell off the boat. As she struggled in the water, one of the soldiers grabbed two boxes that held Mrs. Wetmore's hats. The soldier jumped into the river, and using the boxes to help him float, swam over and saved the woman. The story had a very happy ending: a year later, the woman and the soldier were married. But Mrs. Wetmore lost her hats.

As they neared St. Louis, the Wetmore family saw the *Western Engineer*, one of the first steamboats to travel Missouri's shallow, muddy rivers. Aboard the ship were botanists, geologists, zoologists, and other scientists. Alphonso's regiment would travel with them as they explored the Missouri River as far north as the Yellowstone River.

The *Western Engineer* was designed to look frightening so it would impress the Native Americans. A newspaper called the *Niles Register* described the steamboat like this:

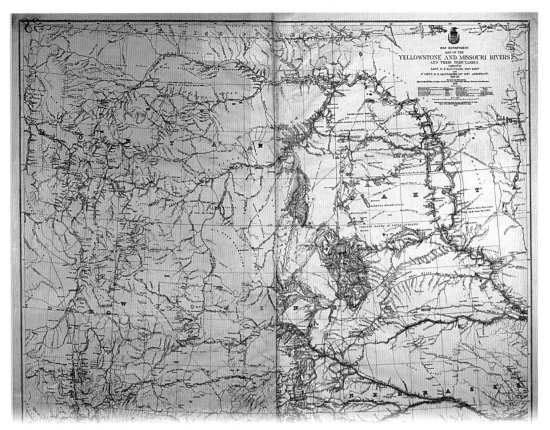

One of the goals of the Yellowstone Expedition was to create a map of the area. Scientists and mapmakers joined the journey to document and map the area.

The bow of this vessel exhibits the form of a huge serpent, black and scaly, rising out of the water from under the boat, his head as high as the deck, darting forward, his mouth open, vomiting smoke, and apparently carrying the boat on his back.

The expedition leaders hoped the steamboat's appearance and noise would frighten the Native Americans, but when one Native leader saw the boat from shore, he asked if he could go onboard and visit!

The Disappearing Town

Franklin, Missouri, was settled in 1816 and by the 1820s was a bustling port on the Missouri River. It was home to Kit Carson, the frontier explorer, and George Caleb Bingham, who became famous as "the Missouri painter." In 1827, the Missouri River changed its course, washing away much of the town. Much of the town's land was lost, so the residents moved to a nearby hilltop and built New Franklin. Years later, the Missouri River changed its course again and the land was returned to old Franklin.

The Yellowstone Expedition chugged away from St. Louis in May 1819 with more than a thousand soldiers accompanying the scientists. The trip was long and slow. One of the steamboats kept clogging up with sand and had to be left behind.

By late September, the expedition had to stop for the winter. They set up two winter camps in the Council Bluffs area. The winter was a terrible time. Cold, wet weather and a lack of supplies led to disease and more than 160 men died.

In the spring, the river rose and the camp flooded, so the soldiers had to move to higher ground. The expedition was abandoned, but the next year, a new fort called Fort Atkinson was built on Council Bluffs, and Alphonso's regiment was stationed there.

While Alphonso traveled with the Yellowstone Expedition up the Missouri River, Mary settled with their three young sons into their new home in Franklin, which was 120 miles upriver from St. Louis. With 800 people and 120 log cabins and houses, it was the largest settlement west of St. Louis.

Mary Wetmore was living on the frontier, but Franklin was a bustling town with stores where she could buy fabrics, food, and other supplies like medicine. There was a courthouse, a jail, a mill for grinding grain, a rope-making factory, a newspaper and printing shop, and a post office. There was a town square with a public well and streets of houses leading down to the Missouri River.

As paymaster for his regiment, Alphonso had to travel year round between Fort Atkinson and St. Louis,

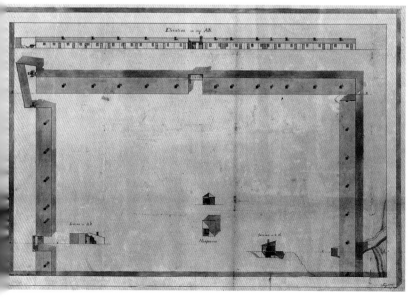

The U.S. Army established forts along the Missouri River to protect traders and emigrants, and to establish an American presence in the new territory.

and could stop to see his family in Franklin. He also traveled east to Washington DC, Philadelphia, and Baltimore as part of his job with the army. He liked to travel over land by horseback, but sometimes he had to travel by water.

Once he had to build a "bull boat," a craft made from a wooden frame and an elk hide. It looked like a teacup. The boat rocked back and forth, but somehow Alphonso floated safely across a stream.

On another trip, he tied two canoes together to make a raft. A terrible storm came up and his rickety craft overturned, dumping Alphonso and his luggage into the river. Alphonso swam to shore, but the money for the soldiers' pay sank and Alphonso was held responsible for the loss.

When Alphonso was traveling, Mary stayed home and ran the household and small family farm. But Mary was not alone. Like many other people, the Wetmore family had several slaves to help run their farm. When Missouri became a state in 1821, a federal law called the Missouri Compromise of 1820 allowed slavery in Missouri and other new states to the south, but not in new states north of Missouri. At that time, even people with smaller farms might have had one or two slaves to help them.

Compared to many soldiers stationed on the
frontier, Alphonso was able to visit his family often.
Sometimes they traveled with him to St. Louis, but
often Alphonso didn't see Mary and his children for
many weeks. When Alphonso stayed at the fort, he
shared a small room with one or two other officers.
When he had time, Alphonso would hunt elk or bear,
or join his friends at dinner, where the men told
stories, sang songs, and put on plays for each other.

Alphonso loved the theater, so he decided
to write a play. In 1821, he wrote *The Pedlar*, using
characters based on his friends and family and other
well-known figures to tell about adventures of Missouri
settlers in 1819. He named the play's heroine Mary,
after his wife. One character was a Revolutionary War
soldier, like Alphonso's father, and another was based
on his friends who loved to hunt and fish. And then
there was Mike Fink.

Mike Fink's Great Shot.

Mike Fink was very tall and strong. Davy Crockett described him as "half horse and half alligator" because of his strength.

Mike Fink was a real person who was well-known for his skills as a boatman and a sharpshooter, and for his pranks and fights. Many people had heard stories about Mike Fink, so Alphonso couldn't resist including him as a character in his play. Alphonso's play was performed in St. Louis, Kentucky, and New Orleans.

Alphonso enjoyed telling about his adventures and writing about them in stories. People back East liked to hear stories about adventure and danger on the frontier, and people all over loved tall tales, which exaggerated events to make them amusing. Newspapers often printed stories—both true and fictional—alongside the news.

Alphonso was one of the first people to write about life in Missouri, and many of his stories were published in newspapers in Missouri and in the East. Alphonso enjoyed funny stories and liked to tell about his own adventures and share stories he had heard.

One of Alphonso's stories was "The Beaver Hunter," which told about a hunter named Mike Shuckwell. Mike lived in Missouri but walked all the way to Nebraska and beyond to hunt.

Mike did not like people, so he lived and traveled alone. As he got older, Mike decided he needed help, so he raised a bear cub. When it was grown, the bear traveled with Mike and carried his pack for him.

Tall Tales

A tall tale is a story with unbelievable elements told as if they were true. Many tall tales use real people or exaggerate real events to make them funny. Mike Fink was a real person who was known for playing pranks and getting into fights. Stories began to spread about Mike Fink, and got wilder with each retelling. People said that Mike Fink could drink a gallon of whiskey and still shoot the tail off a pig at 90 paces. Mike Fink was first used as a character in a piece of literature in Alphonso's play *The Pedlar*.

One day Alphonso invited Mike into his house, and the bear came inside too. As Alphonso watched, the bear climbed onto the bed and settled down for a nap. Alphonso's story was also printed in newspapers east of the Mississippi River, and Alphonso started to be known for his writing and storytelling.

Chapter 4

Trader on the Santa Fe Trail

In 1821, the same year that Missouri became a state, Mexico gained independence from Spain. At that time, Mexico included what is now the southwestern United States. For many years, Spain would not allow American traders to enter Mexico, but Mexican independence changed that. The new country welcomed traders, and Missourians knew they could get to Mexico over land faster than people in other parts of the United States.

In 1821, a trader named William Becknell left Franklin, Missouri, with a shipment of merchandise and headed west to Mexico. He sold his goods in Santa Fe and returned in January 1822, carrying bags of silver coins. When he returned, people came out to hear about his travels and Becknell spilled the coins on the ground for all to see. Word of Becknell's successful trading trip spread and other traders soon followed. The Santa Fe Trail was open for business.

Soon caravans were leaving from Franklin each spring and returning from Santa Fe before winter. Alphonso was impressed with what he heard from traders when they returned from Santa Fe. Missouri Senator Thomas Hart Benton wanted information about the trail and asked several people, including Alphonso Wetmore, to send it to him. In 1824, Alphonso wrote a letter about the route from Missouri to Santa Fe.

Mexico produced almost half of the silver in circulation in the early 1800s, and the Mexican silver dollar, or peso, was recognized as legal currency all around the world.

Santa Fe Trail

It was about 900 miles from Missouri to Santa Fe, and the trip could take more than two months. On the first trading expedition, William Becknell took pack animals, but by 1824, traders were taking wagons so they could carry more goods.

In his letter, Alphonso described what was happening on the Santa Fe Trail and wrote about the importance of the Mexican trade. Because of this letter, Alphonso Wetmore may be called the first historian of the Santa Fe Trail. When Alphonso was gathering information, he was so impressed with what he saw and heard that he took a journey to Santa Fe.

In March 1825, President James Monroe ordered a survey of the road from Fort Osage (near modern Kansas City) to Santa Fe. Alphonso wanted to join that first survey, but he was not selected for the team.

When traders began to use wagons on the Santa Fe Trail, they needed an animal stronger than a mule, so they used oxen, which could pull thousands of pounds. An ox driver used the words "gee" (left) and "haw" (right) to move the team along. The Native Americans heard this, and called oxen "geehaws."

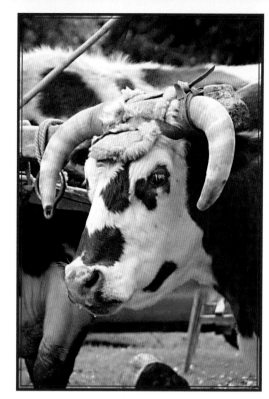

But another opportunity to travel to Santa Fe soon came up.

After the accident in which his boat sank and he lost the payroll money, Alphonso did not have enough money to pay back the army. He needed a way to earn the money. So in 1828, Alphonso decided to try and become a Santa Fe Trail trader. He was granted a year's leave from the army and borrowed money from his father to purchase trade goods.

Leaving Mary and his children in Franklin, Alphonso joined a caravan, a group of traders who traveled together for safety and protection. The group met to decide on rules and choose officers. Alphonso was well known as an army officer, so he was elected as the caravan's leader.

His job was to keep everyone safe and protect the wagons and their cargo until they arrived in

Missouri Mules

Travel on the Santa Fe Trail was difficult. The ground could be rough and rocky or soft and sandy. Near a river or after a heavy rain, the ground could be very muddy. Traders often used mules because they were better than horses at climbing over rocks and boulders. A mule, a cross between a horse and a donkey, can go long distances without water and they are smart enough to know how to avoid trouble.

Santa Fe. Some of the traders did not want to follow the group's rules, but Alphonso stood up to them. Soon they respected Alphonso for his bravery.

The caravan left on May 28, 1828. The trip was long and dangerous. Sometimes Native Americans stole horses and wagons when a caravan passed through their lands.

Alphonso recalled a time when Natives were about to attack the caravan. They formed the wagons into a circle, with the people and animals inside for protection. The Native Americans shot arrows into the camp and the soldiers fired a cannon, and the fight ended quickly.

The weather was another threat. Storms made it difficult to travel, hail could damage wagons and cargo, and a lightning strike could start a fire. Winter travel was especially dangerous because getting caught in a blizzard could be deadly. In the evenings, after the caravan made camp and settled the animals for a night's rest, Alphonso wrote about his adventures in his journal.

He wrote about a long stretch of trail with no waterholes, when his caravan ran out of water and the men and mules nearly died. Alphonso had only vinegar for his men to drink. Some men tried to drink the morning dew. Finally they found a muddy, slimy pond, but they were so thirsty that no one cared what the water looked like.

Millions of buffalo once roamed the plains and prairies of the American west. The buffalo was very important to Native Americans, who hunted them for food, and for materials to make clothing, bedding, and tools. Dried buffalo dung was often burned as fuel.

Mules were brought into Missouri in 1820 and became popular with farmers and travelers because they were strong and hardy. For many years, Missouri was the main producer of mules. Missouri designated the mule the state animal in 1995.

Many travelers on the Santa Fe Trail rode Missouri mules, which were known for being very tough. Alphonso told his friends that one day when he was hunting buffalo, he rode his mule up to the buffalo herd, took aim, and fired at a bull. Just as he was firing, his mule reared up its head. The mule fell over and Alphonso tumbled to the ground. He got up and saw the mule lying still. He didn't hit the buffalo bull, but he had killed his own mule!

Alphonso began the long, dusty walk back to camp. As he trudged along, he heard galloping and braying behind him. He turned around and saw his mule running up to him, ready to go home. Alphonso said that a mule had such a thick skull that even a bullet couldn't hurt it.

Finally, the caravan arrived safely in Santa Fe, Mexico, where the traders were welcomed with parties and celebrations. Alphonso danced with the governor's wife, who thought Alphonso was an important man in the American government.

One night, Alphonso and the other traders were sleeping at an inn when some Mexican troops began a rebellion in the town. The mayor begged the Americans for help, so Alphonso and his friends joined the battle and helped save the town.

Alphonso enjoyed meeting the people and seeing Santa Fe. He traveled for several months far into southern Mexico, where he visited ranches, heard stories about bandits, and saw a church where the stepping stones were made out of silver bars. He learned to speak Spanish and made friends with Mexican families who would visit him later in Missouri. Finally, Alphonso took a ship from Mexico to New Orleans and then traveled home to Franklin and his family.

Chapter 5

Writer and Publisher

After Alphonso returned home from his trip, he returned to duty with the army. Many of his stories about his experiences while traveling back and forth for the army were published in newspapers.

He wrote about visiting Native American villages and backwoods log cabins where he ate bear, deer, and chicken for dinner. He wrote about a time when he was riding in a stagecoach that had to outrun a prairie fire. Another time, he watched a woman use a small dog like a dishcloth to wipe her kettle clean. The dog was fine and went off to play.

Alphonso was forty years old in 1833 when he resigned from the army and moved his family to St. Louis. His education and experiences served him well, and he was able to work as a lawyer and a merchant. He also continued to write and have stories published.

In 1836, Alphonso was a delegate to a convention in St. Louis about the railroads in Missouri. He also ran for Congress, but he was not elected.

In St. Louis, Alphonso met Colonel Charles Keemle, who was a newspaperman, a printer, and a fur trader. The two men decided to publish a book,

In the 1830s, St. Louis was one of the richest cities in the country. Its location on the Mississippi River made St. Louis an important hub for trade and for settlers heading west.

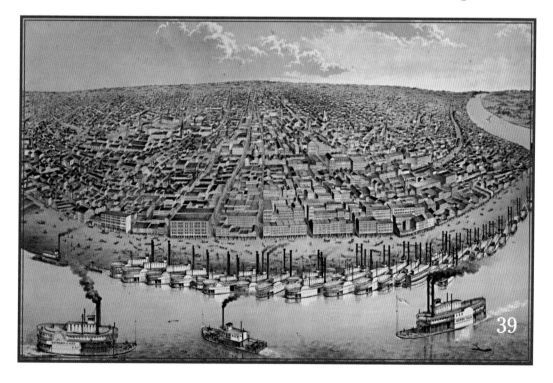

What's a Gazetteer?

A gazetteer is an encyclopedia about a region. A state gazetteer might have a section for each county, with a brief history and information about the geography, soil conditions, towns and population, types of businesses, and available land. When the United States was expanding westward, people in new states would publish a gazetteer to let people back East learn about the new area and to encourage them to move there.

called a gazetteer, to tell people about Missouri.

Alphonso collected information and compiled the gazetteer. It included descriptions of towns and Missouri geography, and told people that Missouri was a wonderful place to settle and raise a family. People who were thinking of emigrating to new territories from the eastern United States could used a gazetteer to help them decide where to live and work. Alphonso was the first person to publish a gazetteer about Missouri.

The *Gazetteer of the State of Missouri* was a success, and by 1837 Colonel Keemle and Alphonso were partners in a newspaper called *The Saturday News*. The newspaper was only a few pages and was printed once a week. It had national news, political discussions, advertisements, and stories of adventure and mystery. Keemle left the paper after about a year, but Alphonso continued writing and editing the newspaper for several more years.

One of his funny stories that showed how pioneers used their imagination was about a fight between settlers and Native Americans. At a place in Missouri called Cote Sans Desseins, settlers were inside a log fort, and Native Americans began to shoot flaming arrows at the wooden buildings. The men used water

By the 1830s, even small towns had their own newspapers, but many came out only once a week. Papers printed a combination of local and national news, plus stories and local notices.

In January 1848, gold was found at John Sutter's sawmill in California. News of the discovery brought thousands of people from all over the world to search for gold.

to put out the fires, but soon the water was gone. They didn't know what to do.

Then a woman had an idea. She ran and got the chamber pots (portable latrines used inside at night) and emptied them onto the fires. After the Native Americans finally gave up and left, the settler's leader was given a new rifle as a gift of thanks. And the woman was given a silver chamber pot!

Alphonso spent the rest of his life in St. Louis with his family. He worked as a lawyer, and also ran a business with his sons. He invested in a mining company, ran for mayor of St. Louis, served as justice of the peace, and wrote articles and stories for *The Saturday News* and other newspapers.

When the Mexican-American War started in 1846, Alphonso organized a regiment, but his regiment was not accepted into the army, so he was not able to serve. Alphonso's son Leonidas joined the army and fought in the Mexican-American War.

Alphonso always enjoyed traveling and seeing new places, so after news spread that gold had been discovered in California, he decided to visit. He traveled to California in 1848, and then returned home to find that St. Louis was in the middle of an epidemic of cholera. More than four thousand people died of the disease between May and August 1949.

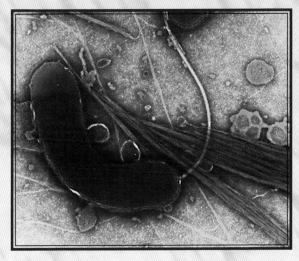

Cholera is caused by a bacteria and is spread through drinking water that gets contaminated with human waste. It wasn't until the 1850s that scientists figured out how cholera was spread. It was another thirty years before scientists learned how to stop the spread of the disease through improved sanitation.

Alphonso got cholera and died on June 13, 1849, at the age of fifty-six. He was buried in a church graveyard, but his grave is unmarked.

Legacy

A Life of Adventure

As a young man, Alphonso Wetmore joined the army and fought in the War of 1812. After losing his right arm in battle, he learned to shoot with his left hand and stayed in the army, where he served as paymaster for his regiment and participated in the Yellowstone Expedition. Alphonso had a great sense of adventure and curiosity, and he did not let his injury stop him from succeeding on the frontier and pursuing a life full of adventure.

After moving to the Missouri Territory, Alphonso was stationed at a fort on the western frontier and traveled for the army. Alphonso wrote stories about his journeys and about life on the frontier. He traveled on the Santa Fe Trail, and wrote an account of trade on the trail. After he left the army, he worked as a lawyer and a businessman, and published a newspaper. He wrote a gazetteer and a play, and many of his stories were published in newspapers. Alphonso's lively and sometimes funny stories help us understand life on the western frontier.

Timeline

1783: The American Revolution ends.

1793: Alphonso Wetmore is born in Connecticut to Seth and Lois Wetmore.

1803: The Wetmore family and friends move to New York State.

1812: Alphonso Wetmore joins the U.S. Army as an infantry officer.

1812: Alphonso fights in the Battle of Queenston Heights, and is badly wounded, losing an arm.

1813: Alphonso marries Mary Smith.

1814: The War of 1812 ends, but Alphonso remains in the U.S. Army.

1818: Alphonso, Mary, and their children travel to Missouri Territory and settle in Franklin. Alphonso is part of the Yellowstone Expedition.

1820: Alphonso begins writing for *The Boonslick Advertiser and Missouri Intelligencer*, a newspaper in Franklin.

1821: The Santa Fe Trail is opened as a direct trading route with Mexico. Missouri becomes a state. Alphonso's play *The Pedlar* is performed in St. Louis.

1828: Alphonso journeys to Mexico as a trader, travels throughout the country, then returns to the army.

1833: Alphonso resigns from the army and moves his family to St. Louis.

1837: Alphonso and Charles Keemle publish the *Gazetteer of the State of Missouri*, a guide to the counties, cities, and towns in the state.

1838: Alphonso and Keemle publish a newspaper, *The Saturday News*, in St. Louis. Alphonso continues to work as a lawyer and writer.

1848: Alphonso visits California after gold is discovered.

1849: Alphonso returns to Missouri, where he dies in a cholera epidemic. He is buried in St. Louis.

For Further Reading

For Young Readers

Dean, Arlan. *The Santa Fe Trail: From Independence, Missouri, to Santa Fe, New Mexico.* New York: PowerKids Press, 2003.

Dolan, Edward F. *Beyond the Frontier: The Story of the Trails West.* New York: Benchmark Books, 2000.

Glass, Andrew. *Mountain Men: True Grit and Tall Tales.* New York: Doubleday, 2001.

Krensky, Stephen. *Mike Fink.* Minneapolis, MN: Millbrook Press, 2007.

Myer, Christopher, and Zora Neale Hurston. *Lies and Other Tall Tales.* New York: HarperCollins, 2005.

Stefoff, Rebecca. *The War of 1812.* New York: Benchmark Books, 2001.

Sutcliffe, Jane. *The White House Is Burning: August 24, 1814.* Watertown, MA: Charlesbridge, 2014.

Websites

American Folklore: Tall Tales. http://americanfolklore.net/folklore/tall-tales/History.com.

"Americans and British Face Off in War of 1812." Video. http://www.history.com/topics/war-of-1812/videos/americans-and-british-face-off-in-war-of-1812

Bean-Mellinger, Barbara, Demand Media. "Why Was the Missouri State Animal Chosen?" http://animals.mom.me/missouri-state-animal-chosen-7686.html

History.com. "This Day in History: November 16, 1821, Becknell opens trade on the Santa Fe Trail." http://www.

history.com/this-day-in-history/becknell-opens-trade-on-the-santa-fe-trail

Missouri's State Animal: The Missouri Mule. http://www. cape.k12.mo.us/blanchard/hicks/Internet%20Pages/ Missouri%20Mule/Missouri%20State%20Animal.htm

National Park Service. "Santa Fe National Historic Trail: History and Culture." http://www.nps.gov/safe/learn/ historyculture/index.htm

Nebraska Studies. "The Louisiana Purchase 'Opens' the West. Other Explorers Follow Lewis & Clark: Stephen H. Long." http://www.nebraskastudies.org/0400/frameset_ reset.html?http://www.nebraskastudies.org/0400/ stories/0401_0111.html

PBS.org. "The Mexican American War." www.pbs.org/wgbh/ americanexperience/features/general-article/grant-mexican-american-war/

Santa Fe Trail Association. "Interactive Trail Map." http:// www.santafetrail.org/interactive-trail-map/

Sources

Barile, Mary. *The Santa Fe Trail in Missouri.* Columbia: University of Missouri Press, 2010.

Benson, Maxine, ed. *From Pittsburgh to the Rocky Mountains: Major Stephen Long's Expedition 1819–1820.* Golden, CO: Fulcrum, 1988.

Byrne, Charles (Lt., 6th U.S. Infantry). "The Sixth Regiment of Infantry." Online at http://www.history.army.mil/books/ R&H/R&H-6IN.htm

State Historical Society of Missouri has copies of the *Missouri Intelligencer and Boonslick Advertisers*, the newspaper that Alphonso Wetmore wrote for.

Index

Image Credits